Chris
MULLIN

Chris MULLIN

SURE SHOT

Terri Morgan and Shmuel Thaler

Lerner Publications Company ▪ Minneapolis

For my brother Jon—Terri Morgan
For my daughter, Kayla Ariel—Shmuel Thaler

Information in this book came from the following sources:
Interviews with Jack Alesi, Warriors conditioning coach Mark Grabow, and
Warriors assistant coach Donn Nelson; The Golden State Warriors media
guide; the St. John's University Public Relations Office; USA Basketball; the
San Jose Mercury News; the *San Francisco Chronicle;* Warriors broadcasts on
radio KNBR, San Francisco; the Associated Press; *Sports Illustrated; The
Sporting News; New York Times;* and *Newsweek.*

This book is available in two editions:
Library binding by Lerner Publications Company
Soft cover by First Avenue Editions
241 First Avenue North
Minneapolis Minnesota 55401

LIBRARY OF CONGRESS CATALOGING-IN-PUBLICATION DATA

Morgan, Terri.
   Chris Mullin : sure shot / Terri Morgan and Shmuel Thaler.
      p. cm. — (The Achievers)
   ISBN 0-8225-9664-4 (pbk.)
   ISBN 0-8225-2882-7 (lib. bdg.)
   1. Mullin, Chris, 1963- —Juvenile literature. 2. Basketball
players—United States—Biography—Juvenile literature.
[1. Mullin, Chris 1963- . 2. Basketball players.] I. Thaler,
Shmuel. II. Title. III. Series.
GV884.M85M67 1994
796.323'092—dc20   94-2704
[B]   CIP
                                                     AC

Manufactured in the United States of America

1 2 3 4 5 6 — I/JR — 99 98 97 96 95 94

Contents

Chris drives against James Worthy of the Lakers in the 1991 play-offs.

1
Bouncing Back

It was crunch time for the Golden State Warriors, the National Basketball Association (NBA) team from Oakland, California. The Los Angeles Lakers had won the first game of their matchup in the 1991 Western Conference Semifinals. Another loss would put the Warriors in a 0-2 hole for the seven-game series.

Warriors coach Don Nelson knew the red-hot Lakers would be tough to beat, especially on their home court. Like the first game, game 2 would be played at the Forum in Inglewood, California, in front of 17,000 fans—with nearly all of them screaming for a Los Angeles victory. Plus, Nelson knew the task would be even more difficult without star forward Chris Mullin in his lineup.

The Warriors had defeated the San Antonio Spurs, three games to one, in the first round of the

Western Conference play-offs. But winning the fourth and final game had been costly. Chris injured his right knee. The injury was bad enough to keep him out of the first game against the Lakers. Nelson didn't expect Chris to be able to play in game 2 either.

Chris Mullin had other ideas.

Like other great competitors, Chris lives to play in the postseason. With an entire season riding on the outcome of a single series, players can't afford to have a bad night. Each game is critical. Some players wilt under the pressure, but Chris thrives on it. He loves matching his skills against the best his opponents have to offer.

But first, Chris had to overcome injury just to get into the game. During the days following his injury, he worked with the team trainer and physical therapist. Slowly, the pain began to subside. Would the knee heal in time? No one knew.

To test it, Chris went to the Forum the day before the second game. Four days had passed since he had hurt his knee, and he was tired of answering the endless questions about his condition. So Chris waited until long after both teams had practiced. When all the reporters and photographers were gone, he put on a knee brace. Then he started shooting around. His knee had improved, but it was still sore.

Even with a sore knee, Chris dominated the game.

The next day, just before the game, he tested it again. This time, Chris was surprised at how good it felt. He told Nelson he was ready to play.

Chris started the game, but he had a rocky beginning. He didn't get even one shot off during the first four minutes. The Lakers took an early lead, with Magic Johnson playing especially well. Then suddenly, Chris came alive. He hit three consecutive shots from just inside the three-point line. After scoring those six quick points, he started sinking nearly every shot he took.

Golden State was trailing by nine points when the first half ended. The Warriors' trainers were worried that Chris's injured knee might stiffen up during halftime. Chris put those fears to rest as soon as he stepped back on the court. He drilled a three-pointer to cut the Lakers' lead to six. He finished the third quarter by driving for a layup that gave the Warriors their first lead of the night, 99-97.

The two teams traded baskets during the fourth quarter. When the final buzzer sounded, the Warriors were on top, 125-124. Chris, who wasn't expected to play at all, had played all but one minute of the game.

"Here is a guy who could not walk, or at least jog, a couple of days ago," Coach Nelson told reporters after the contest. "He was unbelievable."

Magic Johnson agreed. "He was in a dream world," said the Lakers' All-Star. "When God made a basketball player, he made him off Chris Mullin. He is truly an unbelievable player. He's on my All-Respect team."

In the locker room, Mullin was modest, telling reporters the win was a team victory all the way. Tim Hardaway, who had 14 assists and eight steals, contributed 28 points. Mitch Richmond had 22 points, despite fouling out early in the fourth quarter. But the star of the show was clearly Chris

Mullin. He scored 41 points that night, a personal best for him in the postseason. Of the 21 shots he launched, 16 found the mark. He was also 4-for-4 from 3-point range. "That was the greatest shooting performance I've ever seen in a big game," Nelson said.

Chris Mullin was modest, but proud. Three years earlier, a drinking problem had threatened to end his basketball career. He checked into an alcohol rehabilitation center, quit drinking, and recommitted himself to basketball. Chris realized how few people get such a second chance. He had pledged to make the most of his. Now here he was, playing his hardest when it counted the most—in the postseason. Even though the Warriors lost the series, Chris had given each game his best shot.

Chris's accuracy comes from endless hours practicing by himself. Long before he joined the NBA, Chris had a reputation as a gym rat.

2
Keys to the Gym

Chris Mullin is Golden State's most consistent player. His game improves steadily each year, and so does his ability to meet the challenge of a big game. Often, when he's playing hard against a tough opponent, Chris will slip into a mental state that athletes call "the zone." When that happens, he raises his play to even higher levels.

Chris is always one of the top shooters in the NBA. But he gets especially hot when he's in the zone. Then nearly every shot he takes goes through the net. Chris also has outstanding court sense. He knows where the ball is and where his teammates are. Plus, he has an uncanny knack of anticipating where the ball is going next.

Sometimes it seems like Chris was born wearing an All-Star jersey. But what looks so effortless and natural on the court didn't come easily to him.

With dedication, determination, and hours and hours of practice, he perfected his basketball skills.

Christopher Paul Mullin was born in Brooklyn, New York, on July 30, 1963. He was the third child of Rod and Eileen Mullin. Chris's older brother, Rod Jr., is called Roddy by the family. His older sister, Kathleen, goes by the nickname Kathy. His two younger brothers are John and Terrence.

The Mullins lived in a small row house on Troy Avenue in Brooklyn. Rod Sr. was a customs inspector at John F. Kennedy International Airport in New York, and Eileen stayed home with Chris and his siblings. Rod and Eileen spent as much time as they could with their five children. An avid basketball fan and a former amateur player, Rod passed his love of the game on to his sons and taught them how to play when they were very small.

Chris admired his father. He was a warm, friendly man, and Chris felt he could always talk to him. "He would always say, 'Here's the problem, let's figure it out.'"

The Mullins are close-knit. The family regularly attended their Catholic church together. After the service, Chris's aunts, uncles, and cousins would often join the family for Sunday dinner. Chris had a lot of friends in the neighborhood and at school, but his best friends were his brothers and sister. When one of the kids had a problem, the others pitched in to help. When one of them did something special, they all felt proud.

Chris shared many interests with his older brother. Like Roddy, Chris loved to play sports. When he wasn't at school or attending Mass, he usually had a ball in his hands. Baseball was one of his favorite games. As an elementary school student, Chris played on several different church and Little League teams. A left-hander, he was an excellent player at first base and in the outfield.

The Little League team that Chris joined poses for a picture after a successful 1972 tournament. Chris is in the front row, holding the trophy. In the back row, far left, is Jack Alesi, who Chris says "was the first guy who really maybe saw something special in me."

He and his brothers also played stickball. Stickball is a lot like baseball, except it's played with a little rubber ball and a broomstick for a bat. Sometimes the boys would see how many times in a row they could bounce a rubber ball against the front steps (called a "stoop" where they lived) and catch it. These "stoopball" and stickball games helped Chris improve his hand-eye coordination.

When Chris was nine, his father put up a hoop in the backyard. After that, the Mullin boys would play basketball on their private halfcourt for hours during the spring, summer, and fall. In the winter, they'd play inside at local gyms.

The four Mullin boys shared a bedroom. Chris plastered the wall above their triple-decker bunk bed with pictures of his favorite basketball players, like John Havlicek of the Boston Celtics. Chris liked the Hall of Fame player so much that he now wears number 17—Havlicek's number.

Chris admired John Havlicek, who won 8 NBA championships in his 16 seasons with the Boston Celtics. Havlicek also was named to the All-Star team 13 times.

When Chris was in elementary school, he met Jack Alesi. Alesi was coaching the sixth-grade basketball team at St. Thomas Aquinas, where Chris was a student. Chris was just a fourth grader, but he tried out for Alesi's team anyway.

Now head basketball coach at Xaverian High School in Brooklyn, Alesi remembers that year with Chris. "It was my first year coaching," he recalls. "And one of the first things I did was cut Chris Mullin from the team!"

Chris wasn't discouraged. He kept going to the practices, and he badgered Alesi for advice. "He continued to follow me around, and became my sidekick," Alesi said.

Their mutual love of basketball led to a warm friendship. "I ended up playing basketball with him that year as much as I played with my friends," Alesi said. He also started giving Chris tips on the game. "You couldn't show him enough," Alesi said. "Whatever tips you could throw at him, he'd absorb. Even back then he had the determination and overall vision of what it takes to be good."

After that first year with Alesi, Chris was hooked on the game. From age 10 on, he played basketball whenever he could. Between school, church, and local youth leagues, Chris was playing in over 100 organized basketball games a year. He also continued to play a lot with his brothers.

Chris (back row, second from left) was named to his church league's all-star basketball team.

Sometimes when he was playing, Chris would imagine he was a basketball star. He liked to watch basketball games on television with his dad. He especially liked watching the New York Knicks. Afterward, he'd go out to the backyard and practice. He'd work on the stars' best moves until he could do them himself.

"I was a front-runner," Chris told a reporter from the *San Jose Mercury News*. "Whoever was hot that day, that's who I'd be."

When he was in sixth grade, Chris started to shoot up in height. "By then it had become obvious he was a lot more talented than other kids his age," Alesi said. Later that year, Chris proved his shooting ability. First, he won a local foul shooting contest. Then the Elks Club, which sponsored the event, flew him to Kansas City, Missouri, for the national finals.

Fifteen thousand people were on hand to watch the Kings (now based in Sacramento) play that night. The contest was held on the court at halftime. Chris stood in front of all those people and hit 23 free-throw shots in 25 tries. He shot an amazing 92 percent and won the national free-throw title!

When Chris was in the eighth grade, he says, Jack Alesi gave him a set of keys to the St. Thomas Aquinas gym. That motivated him even more than his love for the sport. "I felt obligated to use the gym," Chris said. "So I'd go down there and do these drills by myself. After I started going there alone, I could feel myself playing better. It was the first time I'd ever really felt improvement, and I knew why."

Chris celebrates with a teammate after winning the New York state high school championship.

3
There's No Place Like Home

When he was 13 years old and finishing up eighth grade, Chris faced an important decision. He needed to pick a high school. In New York City, students can choose the high school they want to attend, based on their abilities and interests. Some high schools in New York City offer special programs, emphasizing subjects like science, art, or music. Others are known for their strong extracurricular programs, like football or basketball.

Chris had attracted a lot of notice from high school coaches during the 1976–77 school year—his last at St. Thomas Aquinas. While the attention was nothing like what he would see four years later from college coaches, many of these high school coaches tried to recruit him—that is, they tried to talk him into attending their schools so he could play for their teams.

After talking with his parents, Chris decided to attend Power Memorial High School in Manhattan. The school closed in the early 1980s. But when Chris was growing up, it had a strong basketball program and was well known for one of its former students, Lew Alcindor (now known as Kareem Abdul-Jabbar). Abdul-Jabbar played in the NBA for 20 seasons, won six championships and six MVP awards, and set many NBA records.

More important to Chris than Power Memorial's reputation was the fact that his brother Roddy was enrolled there. By subway and bus, the trip to school each morning took Roddy and Chris an hour and a half. Even with the three hours of travel, Chris still found time to hang out with his friends and play basketball. Popular with his classmates, Chris was also a good student.

Chris starred on the freshman team at Power Memorial. He also made an impact on the junior varsity team as a sophomore. Led by his sharp shooting and unselfish passing, both teams won city championships.

Chris was usually well liked by his teammates and coaches. But in the 1979–80 season, when he moved up to the varsity as a junior, he ran into problems. For the first time, he had a coach he couldn't get along with. Rod and Eileen Mullin had taught their children to respect their elders. Chris tried his best, but the tense situation came to a head during the fifth game of the season.

Power Memorial was playing in a basketball tournament at St. Thomas Aquinas, Chris's old home court. Chris went on a tear, scoring nine straight points in the first quarter. But the coach was upset. He accused Chris of showing off, then benched him for the rest of the game.

That night, Chris talked the problem over with his parents. He didn't think his coach would ever give him a fair chance to prove himself. He also missed his friends from grammar school, and he was tired of spending so much time traveling to and from school. Finally, Chris decided to transfer to Xaverian High School in Brooklyn. By then his friend Jack Alesi had a job there as the assistant varsity basketball coach.

There was one big problem, however. League rules required all transfer students to sit out a year. Chris had to miss the rest of his junior season and the first five games of his senior year. During that year, when he couldn't play competitively, he realized just how much he loved the game.

Chris stayed in shape by training harder than ever. He did a lot of running and played regularly against his brothers at the hoop in the backyard. In the meantime, basketball fans eagerly awaited his return to high school competition. The talk around Xaverian all year was "Wait 'til Chris Mullin comes out," Alesi remembers. "The anticipation and buildup was tremendous."

Chris's first game in a Xaverian jersey came on a Tuesday afternoon when he was a senior. Normally, just a handful of fans would turn out for an after-school game. But on this day, 1,100 spectators crowded into the Xaverian gym. Dozens of people, including several newspaper reporters, had to be turned away at the door.

"For anyone else, the pressure would have been unbelievable," Alesi said. "But Chris came out and scored 18 first-quarter points and finished the game with over 30. For a 17-year-old kid to have that kind of poise was just remarkable."

Alternating between the forward and guard positions, Chris helped lead the Xaverian Clippers to the state tournament that year. In the first playoff game, Xaverian handed a stunned Alexander Hamilton High School team its first loss of the year. "Chris put on a one-man show and we had a monumental upset," Alesi said. More than a decade later, Alesi could still rattle off Chris's stats from that game: 37 points, 19 rebounds, and 11 assists. Xaverian steamrolled through the tournament to become the 1980–81 state champs.

"Chris Mullin was the best player I ever coached," Alesi said. "What he did on the court was a God-

Friend and former coach Jack Alesi presents Chris with a plaque noting Chris's induction into the Xaverian Hall of Fame in 1982.

given talent. But what he did off the court was even more special. He never made excuses, and he never boasted. No matter what, he always did the right thing."

Chris received calls and letters from more than 100 college recruiters around the country. His father helped him weigh the scholarship offers, and the Mullins invited a dozen coaches to visit them. In the end, Chris decided to study business at St. John's University in Jamaica, a community in nearby Queens. The campus was a short commute from his family's house. Chris wanted to keep living at home, and he wanted his parents to be able to see him play.

He also liked coach Lou Carnesecca. "Coach Carnesecca is one of the nicest guys I ever met—honest, always looks you in the eye," Mullin said later. "When you were around him, you got a good feeling about life."

Chris quickly settled into a familiar routine at St. John's. After classes and preseason basketball practice, he'd head home for dinner. After dinner, he would study for a couple of hours. Then he'd return to St. John's to shoot baskets in the gym.

When the 1981–82 season started, Chris quickly established himself as an impact player. The first two college tournaments he played in with the St. John's Redmen were held in front of huge crowds at New York's Madison Square Garden. Chris won Most Valuable Player honors at both.

From his freshman year on, Chris was known for his endurance. He played almost all 40 minutes each game at St. John's. "I never got tired out there," he would say later. "I only wish there were some way to squeeze in a few more minutes."

Chris was a team player, always looking for an open teammate. When he did shoot, his smooth jumpers were a beauty to watch. They were also deadly accurate. So was his foul shooting.

As a sophomore, Chris led the Redmen in scoring. His accuracy rate from the charity stripe was the best in the Big East Conference that year. His steady play netted him a berth on the United States' Pan-American basketball team.

The St. John's University Redmen, 1981–82. Chris is in the back row, fifth from the right (number 20).

That year was also special to Chris in another way. He began dating Liz Connolly, who kept stats for the St. John's basketball team. Soon, Liz was spending most of her free time with Chris at the Mullin family home.

Chris blossomed into a college superstar during the 1983–84 season, his junior year. At the end of the season, he had been named to nearly every All-America team in the country. Then he received an even greater honor. He was selected to play on the United States basketball team that would compete in the 1984 Olympics in Los Angeles.

Chris gets under the basket for a sure two points during the 1984 Olympic competition in Los Angeles, California.

Made up of future NBA superstars like Michael Jordan, Patrick Ewing, and Mullin, the squad beat all eight teams it faced in the Olympic Games for the gold medal. Chris averaged 11.6 points and 2.5 rebounds per game. He finished the series with 24 assists, and his 93 points were second only to Michael Jordan's 137.

After the Olympics, Chris started focusing on his senior year at St. John's. He had already won numerous personal awards. Now he wanted the Redmen to earn national recognition.

Chris got his wish in January 1985. The Redmen had a 17-1 record. For the first time in 34 years, St. John's was ranked as the number-one team in the country.

On March 2, St. John's faced Providence for the Big East Conference championship. Chris scored 18 points to lead the Redmen to a 72-53 victory. The title was theirs! "The championship is a good feeling," Mullin told an Associated Press reporter after the game. "Phase 1 is over, and phase 2 is about to begin."

Phase 2 was the National Collegiate Athletic Association (NCAA) Tournament. Getting into the Final Four was a goal the St. John's players had set at the beginning of the season. The Redmen had been there only once before, in 1952. In 1985 the squad marched through the early rounds of the

NCAA Tournament. Then St. John's faced North Carolina State in the quarterfinals. Chris scored 25 points in a 69-60 victory to help the Redmen clinch its spot in the Final Four.

To his disappointment, Chris's college career ended a few days later. St. John's lost to Georgetown, 77-59, in the semifinals. Despite not playing in the championship (where the additional game would have given him more opportunities to score), Chris led all scorers in the tournament with 110 points.

Chris celebrates with teammates after St. John's big win over North Carolina State.

During his four years at St. John's, Chris set several school records. He was St. John's all-time scoring leader with 2,440 points. He was the school's best foul shooter with a 84.8 free-throw percentage. He played in 125 games, the most ever for a St. John's player. Incredibly, Chris had scored in double figures during 120 of those games. His 211 steals also topped St. John's all-time list. His 453 assists put him second in that category.

Chris was also the Big East Conference's all-time leading scorer with 1,288 points in league games. He was named the UPI Player of the Year and was on every All-America team. Chris also won college basketball's most prestigious honor: the John Wooden Award, given to the best college player of the year.

Coach Carnesecca was sorry to see Chris (nicknamed "Mo") graduate. "Some kids you get tired of after four years," he said. "Mo, I want to keep him around for another four."

4

Dreams and Nightmares

Chris had been dreaming about playing in the NBA since he was 7 years old. Now 21, he sat watching TV in his parents' living room, waiting for the 1985 NBA draft to air. The NBA teams would be choosing college players to play for them. Chris knew his dream was about to come true. Still, he was nervous. Some NBA scouts said he couldn't jump and didn't run very fast. He hoped he wouldn't have to wait long for a team to pick him. He wanted to prove his critics wrong.

He didn't have to wait long at all. Chris was the seventh player taken in the draft, but he was distraught. Chris was selected by the Golden State Warriors, who played in California—clear across the country from New York, his family, and his friends. Suddenly, he felt more like crying than celebrating.

Chris had hoped to join a team based in or near New York. His family and his girlfriend, Liz, were the most important people in his life. He wanted to stay near them. Chris had also gotten used to winning. He wanted to play for a contender—a team that would likely be in the play-offs. Instead, he was headed across the country to Oakland, California, to join a team that had won just 22 games the year before.

Chris and the Warriors took a long time to agree on his contract. So long, in fact, that Chris missed training camp, all of the preseason games, and the first six games of the 1985–86 season. In his first NBA game, Chris made an impact by scoring the winning basket against Seattle. Unfortunately, the season went downhill after that.

Many of the Warriors' players had reputations for being lazy and selfish. When Golden State started losing games, Chris discovered the bad rap was true. The older players wouldn't help him adapt to the NBA. They even scoffed at his efforts to improve. One day Chris stayed after a workout to practice his shooting. "Hey man, are you crazy?" one of his teammates snapped. "You're making us look bad."

The Warriors had Chris playing guard. On the court, he struggled. His defensive moves were slow, so his opponents were blowing right past him.

Chris struggled during his adjustment to the faster, more physical, NBA game.

Chris knew he could score, but the team's game plans gave him few opportunities to shoot.

When he wasn't playing or practicing basketball, Chris was lonely. With his playing schedule, he had trouble meeting new people. He especially missed Liz. Chris and Liz had been dating for three years, and this was their first real separation. During Chris's rookie season, they spent hours talking on the phone. Since Liz also loves sports, sometimes they would both turn on ESPN and watch games together while they talked.

Toward the end of the season, Chris suffered a badly bruised heel and missed the last 20 games. In spite of his shortened season, Chris managed to get into the NBA record book. He shot 89.6 percent from the free-throw line—the second-best mark ever for a rookie.

Chris started all 82 games for the Warriors in his second season. Still very lonely, he fell into some bad habits that winter. In college, he had enjoyed drinking beer with his friends and family. Alone in California, he started drinking beer more frequently. He gained weight, and his game began to suffer. As a second-year player getting more and more playing time, Chris should have improved quickly. Instead, his improvement was very slight. He averaged 15.1 points per game, fourth on the team. His 51.4 field-goal percentage was third best on the team. Chris was disappointed with both marks.

He vowed to get his game back on track. Before he left for New York that summer, he went to the barber for a crew cut. He figured the unstylish haircut would encourage him to stay in the gym, away from places where beer would be served.

But the haircut wasn't enough. Chris kept drinking. He returned to Oakland for his third season weighing almost 250 pounds, 30 pounds over his normal weight. The new coach and general manager, Don Nelson, didn't like what he saw.

New Warriors coach Don Nelson was disappointed in Chris.

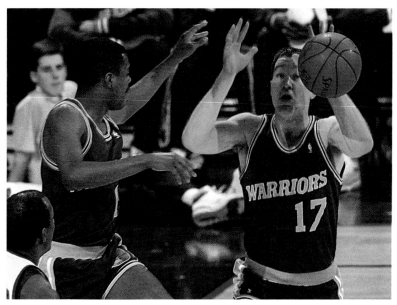
Nothing seemed to go right for Chris.

Chris was drinking so much he didn't really care what his coach thought. He was sloppy, both on and off the court. He was late for practices. He skipped meetings and appointments. "I wasn't happy, nothing was fun," Chris recalls of those days. "To tell you the truth, there were days when I didn't care if I played again."

By December 1987, Nelson had seen enough. He confronted Chris about his drinking. Chris denied he had a problem. "I can't be an alcoholic," he said at the time. "All I drink is beer, and I can quit anytime."

Nelson challenged him to stop drinking for six months. Chris swore he would. The two shook hands on the deal. Less than two days later, Chris broke his pledge. When Nelson found out, he was furious. He suspended Chris from the team. Deal with your problem, Nelson said, or don't come back.

Chris was shocked and scared. He called his parents, and also Liz. With their support, he enrolled in a 30-day alcohol rehabilitation program at Centinela Hospital in Los Angeles. While he was there, Rod and Eileen stayed in a hotel nearby. Chris talked to Liz and his brothers on the phone often. As always, he knew he could count on his family to help him face a difficult challenge.

During his treatment, Chris found out that alcoholism is a disease that sometimes runs in families. Rod, who had quit drinking eight years earlier, was a recovering alcoholic. Chris remembered that one of his uncles had died from health problems made worse by alcoholism. He also learned that his alcohol problems would keep getting worse unless he stopped drinking entirely. "All those factors made it easier for me to accept that Chris Mullin can't drink anymore," Chris told reporters shortly after leaving the hospital on January 29, 1988.

Participating in the rehab program forced Chris to face some unpleasant facts about himself. He had a difficult time admitting that beer had become

Sporting a beard, Chris discusses his alcoholism with reporters at a press conference. He had just returned to the Warriors after completing his rehabilitation program.

more important to him than his career. And that his drinking was hurting his relationships with his family and friends.

At times Chris felt like quitting the program, but he stuck it out. "I remember my dad always said, 'You can always take the easy way out. But the easy way is usually the wrong way,'" Chris said. "I guess I just felt if I did the right thing, I'd get rewarded in the end."

He did. He got his career—and his life—back. "It was the hardest thing I ever had to do in my life, but it was the best thing I ever did in my life," Chris said. "Better than anything I ever did playing ball."

In the end, Chris was glad that Don Nelson had confronted him about his drinking problem. "He brought this thing to a head," Chris told reporters. "He probably saved my life. I'm grateful for him."

A rare moment: Chris watches the action from the sidelines.

5
A Star Shines

After completing his alcohol rehabilitation program in 1988, Chris was eager to get back into playing shape. One of the first things he did after leaving the hospital was head for a gym. "When I was in the rehab center I was thinking," Chris said to a reporter from the *San Jose Mercury News,* "it would seem like a waste if I turned out just ordinary. I wanted to be something more." So Chris began training harder than ever. In less than two weeks, he rejoined the team. He had missed 22 games.

Off the court, Chris made some big changes. He had begun a lifelong fight against his alcoholism. He began attending Alcoholics Anonymous (AA) meetings. He found out where AA meetings were held in every NBA city so he could still attend them when he was traveling with the team.

The Warriors had also undergone major changes during Chris's absence. Golden State had traded several players the day he went into rehab. Coach Don Nelson was reshaping the team, hoping to find the right combination of players to turn the Warriors into winners.

Nelson put Chris back in the lineup for a home game against the Utah Jazz. Worried that the fans might boo or ridicule him, Chris was heartened when the crowd gave him a standing ovation. "The fan reception was great," he said after the game. "But it put a little pressure on me because I didn't want to let them down."

Chris played just 23 minutes, but he scored 10 points, hauled down four rebounds, and got six assists. He also had four key steals. The Warriors won, 102-100.

Under Nelson's leadership, the Warriors improved during the season. Players were helping each other out, and new game plans used the players better. All of a sudden, playing basketball was fun again for Chris. He played hard. His scoring average climbed to 20.2 points during the final 44 games of the 1987–88 season.

Still, the Warriors were struggling. They won just 20 games, and lost 62, partly because of all the turmoil the team had endured early in the season. Golden State finished fifth in its six-team division.

In Chris's first two years with the Warriors, he had raced home to New York as soon as the season ended. In 1988, however, he stayed in California for six weeks. There he began a workout program with Warriors conditioning coach Mark Grabow. When Chris finally headed back east, to the house he bought his parents on Long Island, Grabow came along. For the next eight weeks, the two got up every morning at 6:30 A.M. First Chris would shoot 300 to 400 jumpers. Then he'd lift weights for an hour and a half.

Chris doesn't take his skills for granted. He's almost always practicing.

In the afternoons, Chris would scrimmage with players from the St. John's University team. When everyone else headed home, Chris stayed. He'd launch hundreds of jump shots and free throws until dinner time. At night Chris and his brothers would go outside and play two-on-two until dark. "I've trained a lot of professional athletes, and it's hard for me to imagine any player working harder than Chris did," Grabow said. "He knows where he wants to go. I just point him in the right direction and he does all the work."

The Mullin family in 1984: (front, left to right) Kathy, Eileen, Chris, Roddy, (back) Terrence, Rod, and John.

The next fall, when Chris returned to Oakland, Coach Nelson was impressed. Chris was in great shape, carrying just 215 pounds on his 6-foot, 7-inch frame. He was happier than he'd been in a long time. He was especially pleased after Nelson moved him from guard to small forward. The switch would let Chris play a position that was more comfortable for him. It would also let him shoot the ball more.

Chris had known he would never be a speedy player. Nor could he jump very high. To make up for these shortcomings, he worked on every skill that practice would improve. "If I could slam [dunk] it in, I probably would," Chris said. "But I can't. I had to find another way to score and help the team."

Chris's way was to work on his conditioning, his strength, and his ball-handling skills. "He really squeezes every ounce out of what God's given him," said Warriors assistant coach Donn Nelson. The son of head coach Don Nelson, Donn is one of Chris's biggest fans. "By totally dedicating himself to the sport, he's taken himself from one of the good NBA players to one of the great NBA players," Donn said.

During the 1988–89 season, Chris began to feel more at home in California. The previous June, the Warriors had acquired 7-foot, 7-inch Manute Bol from the Washington Bullets. Bol had played basketball at the University of Bridgeport with Chris's brother John. Chris and Bol had become good friends. When he arrived in California, Bol moved into a condominium near Chris's, and they spent a lot of their spare time together.

Mullin and Nellie—head coach Don Nelson—also grew close. On February 1, 1989, Chris was selected to play in his first All-Star game. There were few people prouder than Nellie that day. "This is an award he deserved," Nelson said. "He'll be a perennial All-Star. He's playing like an All-Pro."

As serious as he is about basketball, Chris usually can find something to smile about on the court.

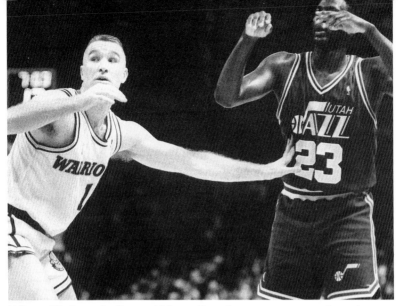
When Chris rededicated himself to the game, opposing players found him to be a much tougher, more effective competitor.

Chris was thrilled. "Every year, even as a kid, I watched the All-Star game," he said. "They're the greatest players in the world. This is the biggest honor for me."

"It's no coincidence that my playing got better when I started taking better care of myself," he added.

To many people, Chris is also an All-Star off the court. In the off-season, he hosts basketball camps for kids in California and New York. He's helped raise funds for the American Cancer Society and the Leukemia Society of America.

"He's really an outstanding person," says Donn Nelson. "It's hard to keep your sanity when you're a star and are being pulled in so many different

With success in the NBA, Chris gets lots of requests for his time. Here, he tapes a TV interview.

ways. Despite all the demands on him to make special appearances, speak at engagements, and sign autographs, Chris keeps everything in perspective."

Chris finished the 1988–89 season—his fourth in the NBA—with 26.5 points, 5.1 assists, and 5.9 rebounds per game. He also sparked the Warriors to a 43-39 record and led them into the second round of the play-offs.

The Warriors rewarded Chris the following September with a nine-year contract worth over $25 million. As a free agent, Chris could have moved to another team. He considered playing for the New York Knicks. In the end, he chose to stay in Oakland. Chris liked his teammates, and he loved playing for Nelson. "He's a great coach who believes in me," Chris said of Nellie, a former Boston Celtics' star.

By then, Chris had blossomed into a team leader. Nelson was thrilled with Chris's decision to stay at Golden State. "What he does for us off the court is more unbelievable than what he does on it," Nelson said. "He gets to the guys. He motivates them, and they adopt his work habits."

Chris jokes with teammate Chris Gatling during pregame warmups.

6
Carrying On

With a new, long-term contract, Chris's future was secure. He could have kicked back and been content with his level of play. Instead, he continued to work hard at improving his game.

"He has such a passion to play," said Mark Grabow. "Whether he was making $2,000 a year or $2 million he'd be out playing ball because he loves it so much."

Always an excellent shooter, Chris averaged 25.1 points per game during the 1989–90 season. The Warriors won 37 games, lost 45, and just missed qualifying for the play-offs.

Immediately after the season ended, Chris flew home to New York to be with his family. His father was dying of cancer. Watching Rod slowly fade away was painful for Chris, and he coped by exercising. He rode his stationary bike for hours on end and swam lap after lap in the family pool. After Rod died in July, Chris stayed busy and looked forward to his next NBA season. "Playing is almost like therapy for me," Chris said. "It's a time when you don't have to think about it."

Before returning to California, Chris married Liz Connolly. Liz also likes staying in shape, and sometimes she joins Chris in his exercise program. Since he quit drinking, Chris has become especially devoted to exercising. He loves working up a sweat riding his stationary bike, running, or lifting weights. He also enjoys swimming, playing tennis and racquetball, and shooting pool.

When Chris quit drinking, he and Liz became even closer.

Chris wipes down his dog, Kuma, after Kuma had joined him for a shower. Chris treats the dog especially well, even preparing hot meals for it.

During the 1990–91 season, Chris put together some amazing offensive statistics. He averaged 25.7 points per game while shooting 53.6 percent from the floor and 88.4 percent from the charity stripe. He finished the season fourth in the NBA in scoring. He averaged 2.31 steals per game that year, also fourth best in the NBA.

Chris keeps a close eye on the ball. His knack for reading the other team's plays helps him get lots of steals.

The Warriors had a good year too. They finished with a 44-38 win-loss record and won their first-round play-off series against the San Antonio Spurs, before losing to the Lakers.

The following year, 1991–92, Chris led the Warriors in scoring for the fifth straight year and sparked them to a 55-27 record. The Warriors made the play-offs, but lost in the first round. Chris's average of 25.6 points was the third best in the league. (In both seasons, 1990–91 and 1991–92, he also spent more time on the court than anyone else in the NBA, averaging 41.3 minutes.)

Chris also reached two important milestones during the 1991–92 season. On December 17, 1991, playing against the Minnesota Timberwolves, Chris scored the 10,000th point of his NBA career. He also became the Warriors' all-time 3-point leader that season.

The previous fall, Chris had been selected to be part of the "Dream Team," a group of mostly NBA players who would represent the United States in the 1992 Olympics. Just two weeks before he began training with the Dream Team, Chris became a father. His son, Sean, was born in June. Like all babies, Sean needed a lot of attention. His diapers had to be changed, and he woke in the middle of the night wanting to be fed. Chris didn't mind the extra work; he was thrilled to be a dad.

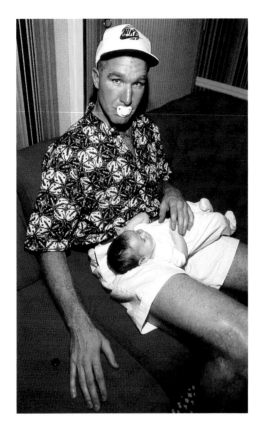

Chris clowns for the camera while holding newborn Sean.

In August, Liz and Sean joined Chris in Barcelona, Spain, for the Olympic Games. The Dream Team won eight straight games—all by more than 30 points—and an Olympic gold medal. Chris played in all eight games and scored an average of 12.9 points per contest. He led the Dream Team with 21 points in the sixth game, as the United States walloped Puerto Rico, 115-77.

Under close guard in the 1992 Olympics, Chris shovels off
a pass.

When the 1992–93 season started, Chris continued to impress basketball fans. He went on a hot streak, scoring nearly 30 points per game. At the same time, he was playing well defensively. On November 7, 1992, he intercepted a pass from Timberwolves forward Chuck Person. It was the 930th of his career, and it made him the Warriors' all-time steals leader.

Chris is almost embarrassed when he's singled out for attention. He'd much rather be known as just one of the team. "The thing I like best [about basketball] is the sharing you do with your teammates, the caring that goes on," Chris said. "It's kind of like what you have in a family situation."

Early in 1993, Chris tore a ligament in his right thumb. The injury caused him to miss what would have been his fifth consecutive All-Star game. Chris, however, was much more upset about missing the rest of the season. The Warriors were struggling. "The pain I can deal with, but not being able to help the team [really hurts]," he said.

Although he would rather have played, he agreed the wisest thing to do was have surgery on his thumb. "I don't want it to get better for a month and then reinjure it again," Chris said. "I have a lot more years to play."

That summer the Warriors acquired Chris Webber, the first pick of the 1993 draft, from the

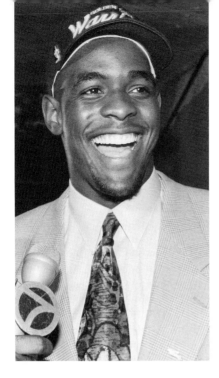

Chris Webber is all smiles after donning his Golden State Warriors cap. Mullin was one of the first Warriors players to welcome Webber to his new team.

Orlando Magic. Mullin was especially pleased about the trade because he knew firsthand just how good Webber is. The summer before, Chris and his Olympic teammates had scrimmaged against Webber and other college all-stars. "Not only was he [Webber] the best player on the development team, at times he was the best player on the court," Chris said.

Toward the end of the off-season, Chris and Liz welcomed a new son into their family. The baby, named Chris Quinn, was born in September.

About a month later, Chris's mother died of cancer. As he had when his father died, Chris turned to basketball to help cope with the loss.

Before the 1993–94 season even began, Chris tore a ligament in his finger that would keep him sidelined for several weeks.

After surgery, Chris resumed his daily routine of exercise to stay in shape for his return to the team. Staying alcohol-free is also part of his daily routine. Recovering alcoholics learn to cope with not drinking by getting through each day, one at a time. Every morning when Chris wakes up, he tells himself, "I'm not going to drink today." Every night before he goes to sleep, he reads from a book titled *24 Hours a Day*. The book inspires him to stay away from beer. He still attends AA meetings. Posted by his phone is the number of a friend he can call if he gets the urge to drink. All these things help Chris stay sober.

Because he takes things one day at a time, like other recovering alcoholics, Chris doesn't like to talk about the future. He says he wants to stay in the game long enough for his children to see him play. He also wants to win an NBA championship.

"We're a lot better off now than we were," he said after Webber arrived. "I feel we're a team to be reckoned with."

CHRIS MULLIN'S
BASKETBALL STATISTICS

St. John's University Redmen

Year	Games	Minutes	Points	PPG	FG%	FT%	Rbds	Assists	Steals
81–82	30	1061	498	16.6	53.4	79.1	97	92	43
82–83	33	1210	629	19.1	57.7	87.8	123	101	39
83–84	27	1070	619	22.9	57.1	90.4	120	109	56
84–85	35	1327	694	19.8	52.1	82.4	169	151	73
Totals	125	4668	2440	19.5	55.0	84.8	509	453	211

College Highlights

All-America, 1984, 1985.
Olympic gold medal, 1984.
John Wooden Award, 1985.

Golden State Warriors

Year	Games	Minutes	Points	PPG	FG%	FT%	Rbds	Assists	Steals
85–86	55	1391	768	14.0	46.3	89.6	115	105	70
86–87	82	2377	1242	15.1	51.4	82.5	181	261	98
87–88	60	2033	1213	20.2	50.8	88.5	205	290	113
88–89	82	3093	2176	26.5	50.9	89.2	483	415	176
89–90	78	2830	1956	25.1	53.6	88.9	463	319	123
90–91	82	3315	2107	25.7	53.6	88.4	443	329	173
91–92	81	3346	2074	25.6	52.4	83.3	450	286	173
92–93	46	1902	1191	25.9	51.0	81.0	232	166	68
Totals	566	20287	12727	22.5	51.7	86.9	2572	2171	994

Career Highlights

All-Star game, 1989, 1990, 1991, 1992, 1993.
First team All-NBA, 1992.
Second team All-NBA, 1989, 1991.
Third team All-NBA, 1990.
Olympic gold medal, 1992.

ACKNOWLEDGMENTS

Photographs are reproduced with the permission of: Brian Drake / SportsChrome East / West, pp. 1, 32, 35, 38, 42, 50; Shmuel Thaler, pp. 2, 37, 45, 48, 49, 52, 56, 64; Peter Read Miller / Sports Illustrated, pp. 6, 9; John Biever, p. 12; Jack Alesi Collection, pp. 15, 18, 20, 25; Boston Celtics, p. 16; St. John's University, p. 26; Ken Weaver / USA Basketball, p. 28; Richard Mackson / Sports Illustrated, p. 30; UPI / Bettmann Newsphotos, p. 40; José Azel / AURORA (© 1984), p. 46; David Strick / Onyx, pp. 54, 55; Andrew D. Bernstein / Sports Illustrated, p. 58; Andrew D. Bernstein / USA Basketball, p. 59; Reuters / Bettmann, p. 61.
Front cover photograph reproduced by permission of Sam Forencich / NBA Photos. Back cover photograph reproduced by permission of Andrew D. Bernstein / NBA Photos.